Chamalú

Chamalú

THE SHAMANIC WAY OF THE HEART

TRADITIONAL TEACHINGS FROM THE ANDES

Luis Espinoza
(Chamalú)

Translated by Sari Bond and Phil Bob Hellmich

Destiny Books
Rochester, Vermont

Destiny Books
One Park Street
Rochester, Vermont 05767

First published in Spanish under the title *Los Pasos del Kaminante*
by Errepar S.A., Buenos Aires, Argentina, 1993

LIBRARY OF CONGRESS CATALOGING-IN-PUBLICATION DATA
Espinoza, Luis.
[Pasos del kaminante. English]
Chamalú : the shamanic way of the heart / Luis Espinoza (Chamalú); translated by
Sari Bond and Phil Bob Hellmich.
p.   cm.
ISBN 0-89281-551-5
1. Spiritual life. 2. Shamanism—Andes Region. 3. Indians of South America—
Andes Region—Religion. 4. Quechuas—Religion.
I. Title.
BL 624.E8613   1995
299'.883–dc20   95–18506
                        CIP

Printed and bound in the United States

10   9   8   7   6   5   4   3   2   1

This book was typeset in Optima with Industria, Lithos, and Modula used for
the display type

Destiny Books is a division of Inner Traditions International

Distributed to the book trade in Canada by Publishers Group West (PGW),
Toronto, Ontario

Distributed to the health food trade in Canada by Alive Books, Toronto and Vancouver

Distributed to the book trade in the United Kingdom by Deep Books, London

Distributed to the book trade in Australia by Millennium Books, Newtown, N.S.W.

Distributed to the book trade in New Zealand by Tandem Press, Auckland

To the Pachamama "tribe" of Argentina,
a precious constellation of people
who make inner growth a celebration

To Domingo Días Porta, a Master

Preface

Beyond words, *Chamalú: The Shamanic Way of the Heart* tells about the process of becoming a Wanderer-Warrior.

From the heart of Andean esotericism, this book is a collection of teachings to be lived and experienced by the Western urban apprentice of our times.

It is not a collection of anecdotes; rather, it is a sequential teaching, which begins with the basic, leading the seeker to the oasis of Sacred Wisdom.

It is extracted and adapted from our life. We have elaborated our thinking for you, the reader, in such a way that this book transcends literary limits and guides you to the pathway of the Sun, so that from this encounter, wherever you may be, whatever your age or lifestyle, your steps also may be those of a Wanderer.

In the oral tradition of the Sacred Wisdom, the teachings are not spelled out. Rather, they are articulated in such a way that the feet gradually become wings and we may begin the transcendental flight to the origins of the Universe.

It is recommended to savor the teachings, following the sequence as presented. The results, without looking for them, will appear in your life, filling it with light.

This is a fundamental call to live with inner power and joy. Our ancestors, the Incas, left us a heritage of wisdom that we would now like to share with you. Welcome.

Chamalú
Comunidad Iniciática Janajpacha
Cochabamba, Bolivia

Chamalú

1

"How would you like to be introduced, Chamalú?"

Shortly after arriving at a certain city where we would be spending several weeks sharing the Pachakuty (Andean shamanic) teachings, our coordinator softly asked this question.

"I am a wandering tree," I replied.

"But I can't say that," protested the organizer. "There are more than a thousand people waiting for you, and many came on foot. We have to say something."

"Then I will present myself in silence," I replied gently. "Those with sensitive hearts will recognize me."

"Chamalú, these people expect us to say something. They want to know the background of the person who is before them."

"We aren't here to give people what they want, but

to give them what they need," I said with emphasis, and before anyone could stop me, I went to the front of the stage. My eyes were filled with people. I felt their presence, their openness, their fervor, as if time had stopped and that moment gave birth to the seeds of the impossible.

As my hand slid in search of my *zampoña* (small panpipes), I asked that those who would dare hold hands and flow with the music, which was filling the hall and the hearts of those before me, moment by moment. Inevitably, the hands entwined, forming ribbons of light. The chairs became unnecessary, as the music flowed through the bodies filled with waves of uncontainable movement. Bodies were freed and fervently broke out of the bonds of conventionalism, etiquette, and false respect that had forced each individual into being his own repressor. Thirsty for love and freedom, they now navigated in an ocean of light.

The celebration had begun. That which had been advertised as a conference had transformed into an overwhelming prayer made of movement, plenitude, and ecstasy. The music and the word, interwoven, flooded those bodies with life.

"Wasimasillay," I said finally, "Brother. It is not necessary to enter into conflict or to burden yourself. It is simply a question of enjoying each day, for in enjoyment we maintain the possibility of learning, and through learning, we grow until we can dress ourselves in light."

At the end, no one wanted to leave. The farewells were warm and endless. Among the many hurried conversations, the words and look of one young woman stood out. When all had finished, she said to me with visible emotion, "Chamalú, I want to go with you. I want to go with you and transform myself. I can't stand another day of my stupidity."

I contemplated her in silence. Her determination was such that I decided to see her the next day.

Eventually, the hall emptied. Even so, the fragrance of the many hearts could still be felt, hearts opening and freeing themselves with tenderness. Grateful to Pachamama (Mother Earth) for this gift, I stepped outside. Once in the street, the same young woman came rushing up to me, agitated as though she had been running. Looking deeply into my eyes, she said, "Chamalú, if you don't come to our appointment tomorrow, I'll kill myself!"

I embraced her in silence. As I left I said to her, "You are at a wonderful moment in your life. This desire to kill yourself reveals your thirst for transformation. You're on the right path, only you have to choose a better method—you have to die in order to be reborn."

I saw surprise register in her face. Visibly nervous, she began to fix her hair, as my words continued: "I will attend our appointment, but not to avoid the unavoidable, not to perpetuate a meaningless life. On the contrary, I hope *you* show up tomorrow, for your appointment is not with a person; it is with life and with its inseparable companion, death. Will you come?"

Without waiting for her reply, I left. I felt that something momentous was about to occur.

2

The young woman was punctual for the appointment. Seated before me, she began to speak:

"Chamalú, I can't put up with my mother and her neurosis any more; I can't stand my indifferent father, who is interested in nothing. I can't stand my sister, who is envious. I get depressed when I think of my ex-boyfriend, who did me so much harm. But forgive me, I haven't even introduced myself; my name is—"

"Your name is not important," I interrupted her firmly. "Also, what has already happened is not important, nor is what has yet to happen. The only thing that matters is this moment, this instant, which instinctively you can enjoy in all its intensity. How are you?"

"I was—"

"It doesn't matter how you were," I said, once again interrupting her. "How are you *now?*"

"I think I'm better, I don't know . . . it's strange."

"The only help I can offer you," I continued, "is to open a passage that will initiate all you want. But this will not serve any purpose if, after sweeping out the house, you fill it up with garbage in five minutes.

"Let's go out to the courtyard. There we will work with pieces of straw. Through transference and with the help of the wind, they will carry away your problems. We haven't come here to carry weight."

We moved to the courtyard and began the work of transference. We asked the brother Wayra (Wind) to carry away the straw, which symbolized the problems. The young woman told me emotionally, through her tears, all the circumstances of her life, while the wind continuously carried away the straw.

When she was finished, I asked her to express how she was feeling. She looked at me with surprise, her eyes still full of tears. Even though she was rigid, the emotions bubbling inside her could not be concealed.

"Don't stop yourself from expressing what you are feeling in this moment," I insisted. "The fears, your thoughts, everything that circulates through the body gets stuck there. Spontaneous movement is a form of liberation."

My words turned into music. The *quena* (Indian flute) and the *zampoña* took turns creating a magic context in which bloomed, from the depth of her being, waves of dead energy, shells of life situations, invisible parasites that usually enter people when circles are not totally closed.

The movement took control of her. Her wailing resounded through the house. Sometimes she took refuge on the floor in a fetal position. Meanwhile, her moans seemed inexhaustible, while her dance of convulsions increased. The cries, blows to the floor, and chaotic movement, even guided by the music, seemed harmonious. The facial expressions, at first deformed, returned to a different normality. Her eyes filled with a special brightness. The music slowly joined the silence. Little by little all that remained was the silence, the peace, and harmony. The clouds in her heart had flown, so that now words could reach it.

"These sounds are seeds," I said, returning to words, "so now the furrow in your heart can sprout, grow, and one day flower. You have to know that we did not come to this world to be unhappy. Life is a school, a precious gift. Through learning and through joy we are able to grow and return to the Sun. Since we can only return dressed as light, it is important that the sacred fire does not go out, no matter what."

"How can I preserve my sacred fire?" she asked.

"By living fully," I replied. "A full life is the passport to eternity. When we learn the Sacred Art of Living, we become Wanderers. The Wanderer is a powerful being, because he lives from his heart."

"Chamalú, I want to be a Wanderer!" she declared.

"The door is open to all," I warned her, "but the path is full of adversities and ordeals, which the aspirant must overcome. It is not easy, because nothing is easy; it is not hard, because nothing is hard.

"It is simply a different opportunity, wonderfully different, an invitation to broaden your limits until all boundaries fall and you can taste multidimensional unity.

"You must have the will to succeed and a lot of courage. Being paralyzed by fear is an enemy. To conquer it is a sacred duty."

"Will the mistakes I have made influence my formation?" she asked, almost anxiously.

"The past is a corpse," I replied. "Don't go through life carrying a casket on your back. Mistakes aren't bad in themselves. If we are conscious, they form part of a valuable teaching. Extract the nectar of what has happened to give you power for the present. The worst we can do is to wander disoriented on the periphery of the present, which each day, upon awakening, we are given. Forget what has happened: the future is only the harvest of the seed you plant in the present. Or I could say, the best way to have an acceptable future is to be happy in the present."

"I want to be a Wanderer," she insisted.

"Remember that the Wanderer is one who has renounced complicating himself," I affirmed. "If you dare to do this, then return tomorrow. The appointment is not with me, but with yourself, through Pachamama."

She left me with great emotion. Her wounds were still visible; energy still escaped from her, but the healing had begun.

"Will you have the courage to continue?" I asked her in my mind, "or will you stop here and, closing your heart, abandon the teaching and go back to your insignificant routine? Will you dare to continue?"

My thoughts were replaced by silence. Slowly I went up to a nearby tree and embraced it . . . and the tree trembled.

Although the rest of my planned activities continued normally, the studies of my unexpected student became a parallel activity, which was thoroughly interesting. It was a new day. She was at my home even before the agreed time. Her manner revealed fervor, enthusiasm, willingness. She was very young, yet beneath her graceful and sensual body was an old spirit rediscovering its direction.

"Where did you study to know so much?" she asked.

"There is a knowledge that comes from a different source than the intellect." We sat on the floor face to face. "Anyone can achieve it who has the willingness, faith, courage, and opportunity to transcend this reality."

"Will I have that opportunity?"

"Is it possible that you don't realize that you already have it?" I replied. "How many people have what they're waiting for, so close, and they don't see it?"

"I'm just afraid I'll never be able to change," she confessed. "My therapist says that some things are impossible to change."

"The spiritual includes the physical, social, and psychological. It rearranges us into our true natural condition," I said with emphasis. "The teaching of the Pachakuty is clear and profound. It is directed to those who trust in their interior potential and who embark on this voyage that liberates—a pilgrimage without complications, without thought, without fear. If you think that this is possible in your case, you will continue to come. If you make your fears and doubts your prison, however, you will keep going back to what feeds your confusion."

"I want to change, but those with whom I live bother me, and I end up bad tempered, resentful, and hateful," she confessed with lowered eyes.

"No one can disturb a Wanderer," I responded, "because he knows that his emotional states are his choice and come not from outside himself but from within. The Wanderer sees life in the form of closed circles. Never leave a circle unclosed; in that way there are no holes through which garbage from the outside can enter. When garbage is thrown at us but doesn't enter, it goes back to the sender, and this is serious. The problem, in any case, is and always will be the problem of who does wrong.

"No one can do harm to you when you are centered, because you are then protected—no one other than yourself, that is. When your stupidity feeds your uncertainty, you start doing and thinking foolish things."

"But Chamalú," she protested, "if they attack me, they harm me."

"No one can harm you when you don't give importance to other people's stuff. They can attack you, and they will, but that's not your problem. It won't have any effect on you if you don't identify with those attitudes, which in themselves aren't violent. But when you give importance to them in a context of fear, they do become poisonous. What is important is that your thoughts and actions are inspired by love. Whatever happens, love is the most powerful energy and the best protection."

"And if they don't respond to love, what do I give them?" she asked.

"You don't have to give them the same that they give you," I explained. "We emit energy according to the vibratory frequency in which we find ourselves, and a loving attitude is the only way to raise the energy of others.

"Being permanently well will enable you to close the circle and to overcome this lamentable emotional condition of a beggar."

"So what should I do when they treat me badly?"

"What do you do when the Sun rises, or when it sets?" I asked. "Well, it's the same. Don't give things more importance than they have; otherwise, you give them power over you.

"Even on a stormy day, if you are to enter the sacred canoe, then you must do it. What is necessary is to make a jump, not tiny frightened steps. Pull strongly on the oars of love and of humor and head for the middle of the river. The shore of success is as dangerous as the shore of failure. Flattery and insults have a common source: those who depend on others. When your circle is left open, you become vulnerable, condemned to crawl rather than to fly."

"But Chamalú," she immediately replied, "if I act that way, they'll think I'm crazy!"

"You are unbearably stupid!" I retorted. "If you care so much about what others say about you, you will continue to fool yourself and lie to them. Modern man is basically a dishonest being, lying as though it were natural to do so and even coming to believe his own lies. If you want to continue on that route, go ahead! But I must tell you that that route has nothing to do with the path of the Wanderer."

"It's also that I don't have a lot of time."

"Typical of the common people," I replied. "In the name of life, they fill their days with frivolities to the point where there is no time left in which to live."

After a pause I continued: "Well, if you don't have time to live, then it's not even necessary to commit suicide. You are already dead."

She looked at me with surprise. Once again her black eyes filled with tears.

"God isn't responsible for your stupidity," I said. "You have made your own prison. You identified with civilization, accepted the garbage it puts out as your own, and the authentic being within you stayed trapped between so much fear and thought. There it is, hidden in a corner, waiting for an opportunity that you refuse to give it."

After a moment of silence, she again said, "Chamalú, I want to be a Wanderer. I'm willing to be one regardless of the price I have to pay. I don't think I have anything to lose."

"That's very true, what you've said," I agreed. "You have nothing to lose, except for the nonsense that keeps you from growing. Your training will begin tomorrow. Come at daybreak."

When she had left, I retraced my steps toward the tree. As I contemplated it, I saw its face smile in a flash of blue light. The tree was dancing.

I remembered the words of the old ones, who said that when one being awakens, Pachamama rejoices.

4

"As of today, your name will be Ajlla." I began our next meeting with a small ceremony of giving her this name. "*Ajlla* means 'the chosen one,' the 'selected woman.' The sacred leaves of the coca plant spoke to me last night about you. You may consider yourself privileged; however, nothing will be given to you unless you earn it. Our work consists merely of opening doors. It is your footsteps that will carry you far, if you are strong and don't give way to the seduction of frivolous and insignificant things in the form of people, whether family or friends."

"What must I do, Chamalú?" she asked, eyes shining with feeling.

"Live, live fully," I replied. "Walk to the top of the mountain. Go forward until your feet become wings. As your vision opens, you will begin to see that you have footprints to follow. When your feet are on their path, you will be in your place. You will be protected. All the Pachamama will be with you. The connection of your ray of light will unite your center with the Janajpacha, superior reality. The Wanderer is wherever he is, but he always lives in his heart. And so, each action is born of love, each thought a vehicle of light. Your subtle bodies will make up the sacred circle. Your presence, wherever you go, even without words, will carry a message."

"I don't understand very well what you're telling me, Chamalú," she said meekly. "Suddenly a door opens for me, and I don't know what to do. I think I will continue making mistakes."

"Ajlla," I said emphatically, "one who learns from his errors hasn't made mistakes. What is important is that each action be an offering, that you are able to transform the profane into the sacred, so that the magic, in the form of light, will purify your mind, and you will become an adequate channel to incarnate the sacred Pachakuty teachings.

"There is no lightning without storms. There is no rain without clouds. Tata Inti, Father Sun, dies every evening; the stars disappear at dawn, yet they are there. What can worry the apprentice Wanderer? Our invisible dimension is immense. We needn't limit ourselves to believing just what we see. Your heart is the best refuge. Ajlla, go to your heart."

"How can I do that, Chamalú?"

"Follow my words. Go through them and situate yourself beyond them. Follow them constantly. It is a voyage beyond reason.

"I am ever the same and ever different. In this new Jatun Pachacuti (Andean era), I am almost six hundred years old; my ancestors live within me. There are things that are not true in this reality, because this reality isn't totally real."

In this way strange words continued to flow, to the confusion of Ajlla—words and then a song, which, mixed with the sound of maracas, produced strange sensations in her. Later, she told me the following:

"I wanted to remain an observer, but it was not possible. The words, the song, the sounds entered me and from within resounded and made me move. I had to hold myself back so as not to dance. At certain moments I was quite frightened, because your face, Chamalú, disappeared, and I saw before me an old Indian who sang very loudly. At other times, I fleetingly saw a group of natives in the jungle dance around a fire. Then you appeared again. Were they savages?"

"They were wild ones," I responded. "The decivilizing process has begun. This is the complete reality."

"I don't understand fully, but I'm willing to go ahead," she said.

"If you try to understand all this from the intellect, you will have entered a blind alley, and your steps will be paralyzed by confusion. Work on these teachings and live them intensely. The light is at the end of the tunnel. It is necessary to keep moving forward.

"Begin your work by observing yourself," I continued. "It doesn't matter what you're doing, just what's going on inside you. In the most diverse of circumstances watch yourself. Turn yourself into a witness of yourself. Watch what happens to you when you are flattered, when you are insulted, when you are treated with indifference. Observe how you feel when things go wrong. Know yourself, but without judgment, without guilt. Just watch yourself, like an explorer arriving at an unknown continent."

After a pause, I said, testing her, "Come back to see me in a month."

Her face registered her surprise. Almost stuttering, she asked, "One month? But you'll almost be leaving then."

"It won't be necessary for you to see me again," I insisted.

"But, I thought that . . ."

Then, changing my tone and taking her hand, I said, "Ajlla, did you understand the teaching? Are you watching yourself? What's happening within you now? How were you a minute ago? How are you now? Do you understand what it means to be a witness of yourself, especially in the worst moments?

"The Wanderer never complicates life. Whatever happens, he remains serene. His look remains loving, his presence fulfilled. He knows that every action could be his last. Therefore, he surrenders totally to whatever he is doing. He always acts from a certain level of consciousness, which permits him to choose his reactions without ever allowing passions to blind his vision.

"Watch carefully how each of your reactions originates. Concentrate on the birth of your moods, always watching meticulously. Your first job is to know yourself. What is there beneath your name? What hides underneath your skin? If you didn't have a name or any way of identifying yourself as a woman, who would you be?

"Your discovery of yourself will make it possible for you to access a full life, transformed into a sacred warrior, a Wanderer of the Sun. Ajlla, tomorrow you will be submerged in the ocean of natural spirituality, where everything is a festival. Welcome to Pachamama!"

When Ajlla left, I glanced at the tree. It danced frantically. The cosmic festival had undoubtedly begun.

I began the teaching of the new day by saying, "When the ancestral spirituality, because of the degradation of man, was changed into a bureaucracy, it became a form without content. It was a grotesque pantomime that no longer moved energy and was administered by people of no authentic inner preparation. The temples then lost their power, thus beginning a despiritualizing process that led to an insignificant, frivolous, super-rational, and materialist human being.

"The energy of the Earth stayed buried within, and the places of power and magic hid their light in the face of such irreverence. Without a doubt there followed a long period of shadows; even our small Pachacuti, five hundred years later, has been invaded by them."

"Were the people of the past more spiritual?" asked Ajlla.

"Magic was the science of the ancients," I explained, "and it was highly developed. Words hadn't monopolized communication. Time was treated like a passageway, and one could take marvelous journeys without the physical body. A common language permitted humans to communicate with invisible beings. Trees, animals, and mountains communicated freely, helping one another in evolution.

"When man doesn't complicate things, nothing is complicated. When man liberates his inner potential, he becomes powerful, and everything is possible."

"Will we be able to become like before?" she asked.

"The Wanderer is the same in all times," I replied, "because his steps never leave the present. And since he is always connected to the source of light, he embodies timeless knowledge and lives not only simultaneously in all times but also beyond them all.

"The Sacred Wisdom of the Andes is not subject to the corroding effect of time. Being connected to the essence, it doesn't lose validity. For this reason, our proposal is not to return to the past but to return to the roots, to the essence. Natural spirituality, naturally implanted in the sequence of our daily lives, fuses the inner and the outer, clothing all our actions in power."

"I have a friend who belongs to an esoteric group, and sometimes when she explains things to me, I find it all so complicated, so enigmatic. The last time I even got frightened," Ajlla confessed.

"There have been times when, because of persecution, the knowledge was enveloped in verbal coverings meant to confuse those who attempted to gain access without proper preparation. There have been other factors. For example, in more recent times there have been people, and many, who entered upon the spiritual path from an intellectual perspective. So they made the explanations complex, overexplaining things and covering them with a curtain of enigmas, totally losing the spirituality that was natural, transparent, alive, simple, and available for all to understand.

"Avoid this type of influence, for now. Listening to those kinds of explanation is like eating a plate of garbage and then hoping for good digestion. The Pachakuty teaching alludes directly to natural spirituality, avoids paying homage to this phenomenon, and uses ceremonial language in simple terms. In its proper time and place, it does not become a distraction causing one to lose sight of the essential. It avoids an excess of explanation. It is not necessary to interpret everything, especially if the intellect intervenes. One needn't understand everything. The sacred path has curves, and when you find yourself on one of those, you can't see what's coming next. You just have to keep going. In that case, you turn your vision within.

"When someone comes to us in search of a return to the sacred, the first question we ask is, 'What would you like to do in this life?' Then the miracles begin to happen. The festival begins. To grow is the most wonderful thing that can happen to someone. Life, without a doubt, is the best idea that has occurred to God.

"Pachamama is a multicolored dance of energy, a date with a rainbow, a declaration of love to a full life. Gradually you start turning into a Wanderer: one who fills the lives of others with light.

"Do you want to be a Wanderer? Spiritualize all your actions.

"Do you want to be spiritual? Start by loving whatever you're doing. In that way, your acts become a meditation, and your life will be filled with power.

"The spiritual person is not the one who wears white clothing, meditates an hour a day, eats only vegetables, and fasts periodically. The spiritual person is one who, having two pairs of shoes, gives one pair to someone who has none. He is a person who shares without waiting for anything in return, who sees a brother, a sister, in the stranger, in the immigrant, in the beggar. It's not a question of following rigid dogmas, of ridiculous fanatics, or of having a group of like-minded friends with whom to interchange smiles and flattery. We find all of that to be abominable. Those who separate themselves from the world aren't spiritual either. Neither are those who isolate themselves, or who make the spiritual path a grotesque showcase. The Wanderer has to know how to live in all realities. His feet should never be separated from the Earth, but his heart should be close to the sky to nourish the inner Janajpacha.

"The Pachakuty is a sacred space fertilized by freedom, where the best of flowers are cultivated and grown, permitting their perfume, in the form of love, to mark the totality of the presence of the Wanderer. Then all becomes a teaching, a caress, a gift. The spiritual, Ajlla, is a festival. Nobody has said to us, Go into the world to complicate your lives, to suffer, to survive in anguish or boredom. In spite of all it teaches, suffering is not our school. Since the school accepts that nothing happens by accident, then we can celebrate everything—everything that happens to us, absolutely everything! Because every circumstance, as hard as it may seem, is a teaching, and the mistakes that teach us something are also teachings.

"We celebrate everything. We are always dancing and singing. Our spirituality conceives of a God who is jumping with joy. It is inconceivable to us to imagine our father, bored, punishing wrongdoers."

"God doesn't punish?" she interrupted.

"The Intij Inti," I replied, "the Supreme Cosmic Energy, has given us a piece of Pachamama to cultivate in total freedom, cultivating the trees of our evolution. The planting, as we all know, is voluntary, but the harvest is obligatory. These are the rules of the game; whether we accept them or not, these are the divine laws. The crossroads of the kaypacha (present reality) in which we find ourselves allows us to go up or down, to ascend or descend. There is no destiny, only tendencies in one or the other direction. Depending on the direction of your steps, things happen to you. There is nothing that we do in this reality that does not have repercussions in the other realities, whence it returns to us with increased power.

"This is where you find the prize or the punishment. God does not punish, Ajlla. It's not necessary, since each one inflicts punishment on himself. Do you understand? In each decision germinates the consequence.

"This is basically good news. Because the possibility to make life a work of art, an endless festival, and a wondrous flight is within the possibility of everyone, now more than ever."

"Why is that, Chamalú?" she asked.

"To incorporate the sacred into daily life there are two fundamental keys. The first of these we see tomorrow," I concluded.

As we parted, our embrace became a dance. From the corner of my eye, I gazed out the window. The tree danced with a white cloud who, sensing a party, had come to join it.

6

"Today we will go to the snow-capped mountain," I told Ajlla as she arrived. "Juan Carlos has lent us his car, and we needn't be back until the afternoon.

"On the mountain lives a very wise old man. We will speak with him during the trip. If you want to say something, please stay quiet. Basically, don't ask questions."

We quickly prepared and left.

"I don't like to drive, but when I do it, I enjoy myself immensely." These were my only words as we departed.

We crossed the city, that deenergizing monster—so many houses, so many things! Where the unnecessary is disguised as necessary, consuming lives. Then slowly the city was left behind. Once again I could hear the song of the birds and smell the Earth. A great joy flowered in my heart, a different kind of joy, the inexpressible sensation of once again being surrounded by beauty.

The asphalt road ended. We continued along a dirt road through small villages until we came to a small mountain with little vegetation. We left the car by one of the small trees and continued on foot. In a few minutes Ajlla's exhaustion was evident. When she couldn't continue any farther, I told her, "Now, take off your shoes and continue barefoot."

She looked at me in surprise, and seeing my expression, which reflected my wishes, she quickly became barefoot and continued.

Soon we saw, at the end of the path, a small rustic house. As we drew near, an old man came out to receive us and, without speaking, invited us to sit on a large old log at the door of his house.

"Ajlla," I said as I sat, "you may stay or go for a walk. You decide, in complete freedom."

She stayed, thinking to take part in the conversation, but she soon realized that words were not being used. We remained in total silence for several hours. At times Ajlla would go walking and, upon returning, would find us as before, in silence. In the afternoon, after sharing some food, we parted, still in silence, and began the journey home.

Ajlla could no longer contain her need to ask questions. Her large eyes were filled with curiosity and emotion.

"Now you may make use of words," I said. "Would you like to say something?"

"Will you answer with words?" she asked, intrigued.

"For a short time more we will continue using words," I replied. "But the day will come when they will no longer be necessary, when distance will no longer be an obstacle. Actually, there's very little to explain; however, ask whatever you like."

"Why didn't you speak at all with the old man?" she immediately asked.

"Of course we spoke," I replied. "We just didn't use words."

"I don't understand."

"I'll have to explain to you in silence."

"Chamalú," she insisted, "I want to understand everything, but without the use of words, I fear I will understand nothing."

"Ajlla," I said, taking her hand, "now we depend on words, in the same way that we depend on this car at this moment. Later, neither the car nor the words will be necessary."

We sat for some time in silence as the car carried us to the city.

"In ancient times," I eventually continued, "our ancestors did not need to speak in order to communicate, nor did they depend on technology outside of themselves. Many other capacities were available then. The 'supernatural' was part of the natural. Everything was different. God wasn't confined to temples, nor was the everyday separate from the sacred. We spoke to the Earth, and the common language of all beings, visible and invisible, was accessible to all. Everything was so different."

"You speak of that time with nostalgia, as though you were there," Ajlla said.

"I was there a short while ago," I confessed. "And before, I also lived in those unforgettable circumstances. Things are cyclical, Ajlla. Life is a river that circulates through this and other realities. When the river ceases to flow here, it continues in other ways, because there are other 'heres.' This is hard to grasp, and even more to truly understand. Vision clears, and understanding comes from other sources."

"Who was that old man, and what was he telling us?"

"He spoke to us both, and he spoke very well of you to me. He is my younger brother."

"Your younger brother!" she exclaimed. "How old are you, Chamalú?"

"Years only serve to calculate chronological, linear age. For many years I have walked this land. Soon I will leave."

"Are you referring to dying, Chamalú?"

"Ajlla, death does not exist," I said slowly. "It is the dawning of a new day, birth into new life. For this reason, our ancestors buried their dead in the fetal position, in festive dress and with their heads to the west. Everything is cyclical. Life is circular like the nest of the birds, like the trunk of the trees, like the face of Tata Inti."

"Where do we go when we die?" asked Ajlla.

"Life continues in another form," I clarified. "Each night when we sleep is a small practice. It is a short death. Every awakening is a resurrection, which we celebrate.

"Never go to sleep," I continued, "without having forgiven everything, without having purified yourself. In that way, you will always be ready, prepared for death. This is what life is: the preparation for death. The best way to prepare for that inevitable day is to live well, making each day an opportunity to grow and to give thanks. Make each act an act of love, each thought a ray of light.

"Side by side with our canoe flows the transparent canoe of death. It is always there. There are those who feel fear, but it glides beside us to remind us that today we are to live."

"Does all this have something to do with the old man we visited?" she asked.

"Today, I wanted you to understand the value of silence, as a context that gives access to other realities," I replied. "That old man we visited died several years ago, but that's not what's important, just the silence."

"But . . . then who were we with? Chamalú, I don't understand."

"Ajlla, your intellect is not the destination of this

teaching. There are things that are not true in this reality. The place we visited is not real in this reality, but it is real in the other."

"But—"

"No, Ajlla," I said, cutting off her question. "When silence is total, it permits us access to a knowledge that is right here, like the voice of the radio when we turn it on. We simply need to have the apparatus that gives us clear access."

"Ajlla," I concluded when we arrived in the city, "when you visit other places, it's important to bring absolutely nothing back with you. The only thing permitted is the teaching. I can verbalize the teaching only this far; the rest will germinate in you at the right time if you permit the silence to fertilize the seeds of wisdom. The other key we will see tomorrow."

A silent embrace concluded the teaching of that day.

"I love your fervor, your willingness, your immense desire to grow, Ajlla," I said at the start of the new day. It moved me to see her arrive running, enter the house with her usual timidity, and sit down in silence, always in the same place.

"Yesterday, you discovered that the Pachakuty teaching is beyond words," I continued, "and even though I hadn't explained anything to you, the teaching could not be interrupted. When we stop learning, we are dead. Each instant is an opportunity to learn. Then we can go beyond reason. Then the commitment to life and to the spiritual will have been initiated simultaneously."

"Chamalú," Ajlla interjected, "I understand your teaching better all the time. But at times, for example, when you take my hands or when you embrace me, I forget everything, and I start to tremble like a little girl."

"It's that you are a little girl, growing intensely," I replied. "Western man lives in luxurious prisons built by himself: prisons of rules, prohibitions, dogmas, and his own thoughts, over which he has no control. In this sad circumstance, spontaneity, purity, love, and innocence are sacrificed. He prefers to run in desperation rather than enjoy the walk. Caresses have been forgotten in personal relationships, because tenderness, having no value, has been suppressed. The contact we will eventually have is a call to spontaneity, to purity, a remembering of the beauty of life and the importance of falling in love with it."

"And if I fall in love with you?" she asked, her eyes shyly lowered.

"When you discover life, it is inevitable that you will fall in love with it," I answered calmly. "I am just the bridge that permits you to cross the river and reach the shore of wholeness.

"And confusion is merely through association. Fall in love with life and decide to be faithful, no matter what."

"What does it mean to be faithful to life?"

"The only way to be faithful to life is to be happy," I answered. "Joy is our natural condition and the main symptom of finding our true place.

"Love whatever you do," I continued, "no matter how insignificant. Love intensely and unconditionally. The love you embody will harmonize you.

"Basically, love in the worst moments. There is no better protection than tenderness. There is no better fuel than love. Living without love is like a car without gasoline. Those who love become powerful, and miracles happen to them daily.

"Ajlla, to live means to love, to be alive means to be loving. The capacity to love means loving without expecting anything in return. Decide to live and to love. One who loves what he does is doing what he loves, and that's wonderful. The enemy of love is fear. Love begins when fear ends. There are no braver beings than those who are able to love unconditionally. To love is the best prayer; the rest is insignificant words. If we simply love, our days will be filled with light.

"We have to be careful that no one interrupts our loving. The Intij Inti is always at the side of those who love . . ." I stopped suddenly, seeing that Ajlla was crying.

"I am crying," she said, responding to my unspoken question, "because all that you are saying is the exact opposite of what I have done in my life. How can I keep from crying when I've been walking in the completely wrong direction, Chamalú?"

"Nowhere can you find a better refuge than in loving," I continued. "One is never as strong and as powerful as when one is loving, no matter what else is happening. The love I speak of is that powerful energy that is capable of transforming lives and healing the sick, a love that has nothing in common with the sentimental, weak, and dependent attitude of those who say they love but are full of fear and mistrust. It has nothing in common with the sentiment that suddenly ends or turns into resentment, or that chains the other. The love of which I speak is freeing, healing, total.

"At the heart of each person lives a being that is immensely loving. When this being is free, love flows spontaneously, filling us with light. We would not have to make ourselves love, or even learn how to love, if we had not suffered such a grotesque deformation of love. Let us hope that modern man will stop torturing his children, converting them into repressed beings incapable of giving or receiving love, who for that reason go through life empty of tenderness, hungry for affection, who at the slightest caress don't know whether to be grateful or angry.

"There are those who think that love should be reduced to the couple exclusively. Actually, love should fill all the chapters of our lives in its purest form. Cosmic love is the authentic path of purification. On this path, there is no need for labels or thoughts; life becomes a luminous flow, intensely liberating, establishing the most imperturbable inner peace.

"If people would understand that they need only

love, they would stop running after false goals, stop burdening themselves and complicating life. He who loves himself and others is immunized against many illnesses, free of anxiety, fear, and unstable thoughts. Love converts us into channels of the most powerful cosmic energy. In this way, supreme ecstasy becomes a daily occurrence, and the imprisoning limits of this little reality are transcended. Life's experiences become inexpressibly lovely; and so we recognize our essential identity: we were just love, volcanoes of love waiting for liberation."

"If we are full of love," asked Ajlla, "why is the first thing that comes out of most people either irritation or anger?"

"Underneath the cement, the Earth is warm and fertile," I replied. "In the same way, modern man has been asphalted with prejudices, with fears, with garbage in the form of education. And so, when he is faced with adverse circumstances, the first thing to emerge is the muck. Even so, at the core there remains a loving person, in this case cornered, tied, and muzzled by chains of endless thought.

"The Sacred Art of Living is in direct relationship to the capacity to love unconditionally, even in the most diverse circumstances. When we love, our feet become wings and our walk a wondrous flight."

"And if others don't return my love?" asked Ajlla.

"That's not important, Ajlla," I explained. "What's important is what you give, not what others give. No

beggarly sentiment is important. The best way to receive love is to love without expecting anything in
return; to love is to plant seeds. The harvest isn't
immediate. What's important is to enjoy the planting,
not to be thinking of future harvests.

"There are those who want to love, but only under
predetermined conditions. Authentic love flows in
torrents, with no conditions added. Also, a little love
doesn't work, because it is fragile and perishable.
Anyone can break a small branch of a tree; one tree
is already stronger, and a million trees together . . . We
need this dimension of love. Only a tremendously
loving person is truly powerful.

"The inability to love is the path to unhappiness.
There are very intelligent people who live in misery
because they neither love nor receive love. What
perpetuates this sad state is that they can't admit to
their incapacity to love, and so it continues, decorated
by elegant words and hypocritical smiles.

"The love that you give is the best message, the
most beautiful discourse, the most authentic teaching.
Why does it matter if your love is not returned? Have
you forgotten that one can give only what one has?

"Actually, your love will make it possible to understand those who are incapable of love. Moreover, you
must not judge these people; you must help them,
lovingly. We can retrieve love not with words but only
by loving even more.

"When you are love, and love is you, the circle is

closed. Your harmonic vibration will connect you to levels of protection, you will be in your true place, and your loving presence will be the best possible present to those around you.

"Unconditional love is the other key."

When Ajlla had left, I went out to the garden and placed my hands on the ground. Even though I was in the middle of the city, I could feel the heartbeat of the Earth. I felt her love, her life. I felt as if roots came out of my hands, I felt the tender embrace of Pachamama, Mother Earth, who continues to wait for the reverent return of her children.

Today I received Ajlla in an unusual manner. Without words, my hands spoke through caresses, while she, surprised and pleased, remained still. My fingers played with her hair, which whimsically fell in waves, covering almost her entire back in careful disorder. When my hands rested on her shoulders, the caresses became a massage, which gradually extended over the whole of her body.

"Thank you, Chamalú. I feel so rested now." These were her first words.

"How many people go through life without ever receiving a massage," I commented. "When the hands express themselves, and do so lovingly, like flowers giving off perfume, they transmit an energy so profound, so capable of healing, harmonizing, and energizing, that words are incapable of describing the process.

"The hands of a loving person are incredibly powerful and healing. There is nothing more comforting and agreeable as caresses.

"How do you feel now?"

"Very well, better than ever, although at the beginning I was a bit surprised," answered Ajlla.

"Physical contact has been erased from the life of modern man," I said. "He has reduced his communication to verbal forms, which, while not lessening the distance, makes communication cold and superficial.

"In our communities, physical contact is a way to know others. Caresses form part of daily life, in that precious state of innocence that frees us from interpretation or other unnecessary explanations. If each person were able to open within himself a zone of light, freed from all thoughts, then interpretative and thought-filled nightmares would cease. This would once more give innocence the sacred context in which spontaneity flows freely, fully, and totally. Paradise is not in the future or far away. Innocence and beauty are privileged refuges. There, the light is more intense. From there it is possible to love everything and in freedom; so everything acquires a different connotation. Love is inevitable and joy unbearably beautiful.

"I feel the need to love," I continued, "to love everything, to share love, because it is possibly the only thing in life that the more you give of it, the more it multiplies. I declare my love for the world. As proof of this, we who embody the Pachakuty knowledge don't evade life, don't isolate ourselves, don't leave the cities. The presence of Wanderers is necessary in all places. If we know how to be complete and invincible, we will encourage the inclination toward a superior life, and the most wonderful journey will have begun.

"Do people dress themselves to cover their bodies or to hide them?" I asked suddenly.

After a moment of silence I continued, "Surely, it is not only climate or esthetics that determines one's clothing; rather, it is shame that we feel for certain parts of the body.

"When we are children, innocence is our normal condition. Little by little, the process of incorporation into society teaches modern man to feel shame through prohibitions, threats, and punishments. Little by little, the child reproduces the defects of the adults. Spontaneity and purity remain suppressed; innocence is no longer acceptable. Almost everything becomes grotesque, calculated, and filled with bad intentions. When we feel shame for the body, we start to hide it. In hiding it, curiosity is awakened; it is forbidden to be seen, and the forbidden is sought by all of us, in many cases becoming an obsession. The naked body, in a state of purity, is the most natural, lacking any sexual or pornographic intent. It is a gesture of freedom and innocence.

"Originally, our brothers and sisters in the jungle did not dress themselves. This seemed unbearably obscene for the morbid priests who, with effort and bad intentions, succeeded in teaching them to feel shame, to hide, and to prohibit. Indirectly, this led to a wide variety of sexual crimes, which had not existed previously among the indigenous peoples.

"We must not forget that we were born naked and that before the sacred Intij Inti we remain naked.

"When you dress, Ajlla, don't be influenced by style, which enslaves; don't dress out of shame for your own body, or to please others. Choose clothing of natural fibers that is comfortable and pleasing to you; let your clothes adorn your body so your freedom may be preserved. Outer beauty is little more than a complement to inner beauty. Beauty has more to do with love and joy than with sophisticated procedures that make you appear different from who you are.

"The cleansing of the body is a meditation and a ceremony. We have a duty to keep our corporeal vehicle strong, healthy, harmonious, and fulfilled. We are not *only* the body; we are *also* the body. At any age, we have to keep the body agile and in good condition. This has to do with both external and internal hygiene. It is not hygienic to wear too much clothing and never to walk barefoot on the Earth. It is not hygienic to have vices, addictions, or negative thoughts, because what we think does not stay in the head. Our negative thoughts circulate throughout the body and stay there, contaminating it."

"Are purity and innocence possible in a society as corrupt as today's?" asked Ajlla.

"The innocence we proclaim has nothing in common with stupidity," I affirmed. "Purity is one of the characteristics of the Wanderer, his refuge and his strength. When we speak of purity, it includes the sense of ubiquity. That lucidity makes loving attitudes possible, inspired by the highest sentiments.

"To be indigenous, to be wild in this new Pachacuti," I continued, "means to be children again. When we are again childlike, we aren't interested in diplomas or applause, in appearances or in gratitude, but only in a life full of action, because everything then becomes a sacred play.

"The children of the Earth recognize innocence as their natural condition. That's why they do not fear caresses, nor are they frightened of spontaneity. They are humble and gentle. They don't seem to know much, but you feel in their innate clarity that wisdom is part of the natural condition, as heat is to the Sun. Purity guarantees total action. Your actions then become circular, and the opinion of others is no more important than the leaves blown by the autumn wind.

"Be yourself, Ajlla. Liberate your freedom. Allow your spontaneity to manifest itself throughout your body. Contemplate life with eyes of purity; then, wherever you look, you will see beauty."

From that moment on, everything became a language of silence, looks, and caresses, as if two children were playing with their friend disguised as a tree, under the joyful gaze of Father Sun, who was also celebrating with us.

In the morning, without leaving my room, I sent one of the boys of the house to tell Ajlla that I was not home.

"But we were supposed to meet at this hour!" she exclaimed, in surprise and anger.

"Chamalú said that since he was free today, he would go out to the country and return late," continued the boy, who had been told what to say.

"It's not possible that he has forgotten me," protested Ajlla. "For over a week I have come every day at the same time."

"That's all I can tell you," insisted the boy coldly as he was leaving. "If you want to wait all day, you may, but in the courtyard."

Ajlla did not move, apart from her rapid and broken breathing. Her eyes remained fixed on the floor as she thought, "Chamalú left without caring how his attitude would make me feel. He's selfish, he's . . ."

And her thoughts spun on, confused, unstoppable, out of control. She sat on the edge of her usual seat, folding her hands and staying quiet, as the slow passage of time was marked by an antique clock on a nearby wall.

A few hours later I entered the room, and almost without looking at her, I said, "You were right to stay here, but you were wrong to get angry and lose your harmony. Why did you stop moving from your heart? No, Ajlla, you won't get far if you are not able to maintain your balance in the most varied of situations. Humor is the inoculation against stupidity and illness; humor is the guarantee permitting clarity; humor is an important step in the pilgrimage of the Wanderer. Where would we be without humor? How is it possible after so many teachings that you still complicate life? Ajlla, there is a great truth that you must always remember: the only serious thing in life is humor.

"When you lose humor, your invincibility suffers. And when that cracks, you become totally vulnerable. You can only remember humor in the context of humor. Otherwise, it will quickly dissolve, and instead of flying, you'll once again be crawling miserably.

"Ajlla, eternity is nothing more than the moment fully experienced. The infinite fits into the heart of the Wanderer. We just have to remain true to humor and then our harmonic vibration will expand without stopping. Even if we do nothing, our presence will be a valuable contribution.

"When a wise man starts thinking, he becomes foolish. When a Wanderer becomes angry, he can no longer fly but only crawl miserably. Ajlla, open your heart and start to play. Never, under any circumstance, lose your sense of humor. Where would we be without humor? How can you not be grateful to be part of the wondrous Pachamama; how can we forget that we come from the sacred Intij Inti? Ajlla, sow seeds of love, and you will harvest joy. When we are happy, our cells are singing and a profound peace floods our body. With the eyes of the heart, we see that the birds don't fly but are dancing in the air.

"Ajlla," I continued, "we, the indigenous people of the new Pachacuti, are like the rain. We have come down to the world of modern man to remind him through our example and our gentleness that it is only a question of flowing, that flowing is how we find the path to Janajpacha. This transformation raises our vibration, allowing for qualitative change indispensable to our evolution.

"This process would not be possible without humor. Ajlla! If you cannot respond unperturbed and harmoniously, the Wanderer will have aborted. In the worst of circumstances, your well-being must be preserved; then you can continue acting from a certain level of consciousness; then your pending voyage will take place permanently—the voyage within.

"If nothing happens by accident, why complain? Why get angry, if nothing happens without a reason? Everything is a teaching. Therefore, learn gratefully, accepting everything naturally. You only need to be well. Everything else will come of itself.

"When life has no meaning, our reactions become aggressive and out of control, even if nothing hurts us. We look for justifications, or we blame someone else. But when shamanism is our way of life, everything becomes something wonderful and humorous.

"In our native genesis, the Intij Inti told us: 'Go out into the world to enjoy yourselves, because in enjoyment you learn, and in learning you will grow, and in growing you will fulfill the sacred reason for evolution.' Why not replace doctors with humorists in the hospitals? Why not plan humor groups every weekend? Why not have a moment for humor every day, wherever we are? Why not perpetuate this moment and make our lives an act of uninterrupted sacred humor?

"Ajlla, we have been given the capacity to laugh at ourselves so that we *can* laugh at ourselves—to smile when things turn out as we wish and especially when they turn out differently. If you do something wholeheartedly and enjoy the effort, it's all right. The outcome is unimportant. What counts is what has been learned.

"We have been given the capacity to laugh at ourselves, especially so that we can laugh at our mistakes.

This healthy joy permits us to preserve the clarity necessary for the learning, which is to say, the growing, to take place.

"Ajlla," I said, giving her an embrace, "if your heart is smiling, your face will not grow dark, no matter what happens. And when the night comes, you will be the light. And when humor is present in the worst moments, the Wanderer begins to take form, which is to say, the celebration is guaranteed, for every act is a celebration."

We parted with joy. The tree already knew: what would become of us without humor?

10

"We are as important as stones," I began the new day's teachings. "In ancient days, the gods gave us an important gift: life, a sacred ground in which to cultivate the most beautiful flowers, the most impressive trees. They gave each of us the same present in different wrappings; pieces of Pachamama are available to those who feel the transcendental reasons for our passing through this planet. Everything is alive, everything is enrolled in the school of evolution. Everything is people in different clothing. One day, everything will become a star again.

"When a person is still asleep, he acts out of pride. Arrogance is his calling card, his presentation. What sadness Pachamama feels to see how her children have gone astray. How often the doors to the Universe close on those who are missing the magic passport of humility! Ajlla, arrogant people are prisoners of their own stupidity. They say strange things, which come from the thoughts that ceaselessly fool them. Often they think of themselves as 'good people.' They have the tendency to attribute to themselves a large quantity of virtues, abilities, and teachings that convince them of their superiority over others. All of this translates into a true prison cell, invisible but totally efficient in allowing them to express foolishness. If four vain people take a corpse to the cemetery, in truth, there are five dead.

"The other big problem that arises from a superior attitude is that this type of person, while he maintains this ugly attitude, is condemned to live exclusively in terms of this reality, closing a sad, vicious circle that feeds off its own foolishness.

"Arrogant people are inevitably foolish, because they evaluate everything according to their own standards. Everything is good or bad according to how it seems to them. Their lives are a disagreeable routine, because they are forever comparing themselves to others. They base their decisions on the distorted image they perceive from their surroundings. The arrogant live lives of suffering, because they have replaced inner growth with ridiculous competition to be better than others; thus they are permanently tense and rushed. This hurry, this obsession keeps them from enjoying what they have. Not being happy, they become ill. For this reason, their aspirations are always low: materialistic, frivolous, insignificant, even when they take part in the spiritual world. Coming with all their garbage, they continue to reproduce the same faults and, in consequence, are not able to understand anything. Their spiritual practice becomes a grotesque mockery, of which they are the principal victims.

"It is impossible to have access to the sacred language of Pachamama if one is lacking in humility. Arrogance and vanity are the total opposite of the Way of the Wanderer. There is no way to access the knowledge without the primary requirement of humility, but by having it, we can enter into all realities, all dimensions. Humility, Ajlla," I continued, "is for us a qualitatively different vibration. One who is humble gradually becomes strong and powerful. Only those who purge themselves of fears can be truly humble. Humility is basically an act of courage."

"Why is it so hard to be humble, Chamalú?" asked Ajlla, with obvious interest.

"How many times have you asked me the same thing?" I responded. "Modern man finds it especially difficult. It seems to have something to do with the education received from family and school, where one is taught to be individualistic, egoistic, and not responsible for others. Modern man is taught to compete rather than to share, and there he is, competing and running until a heart attack takes him out of this infernal race.

"The lack of humility acts as a blindfold over the eyes of the soul. The arrogant go through life unaware of most things.

"Ajlla," I said, suddenly changing my tone, "you are one of the worst students I have."

"Chamalú!" she exclaimed in surprise, "why do you say that?"

"So that you won't be infected with vanity, or corrupted by pride," I replied. "The key of the Wanderer is humility."

"Please, tell me more about humility," she asked, more and more motivated by the subject. "How should I act when I'm confronted with someone who acts from hypocrisy? Wouldn't my humility be an approval of such conduct?"

"Ajlla," I responded slowly, "I said previously that humility does not signify stupidity. It has nothing to do with a foolishly fearful attitude. On the contrary, it is the bravest attitude, because only those who are filled with courage can truly be humble.

"To be humble is to walk with the heart. When you find someone with an erroneous attitude, do not take advantage of the opportunity to humiliate them, nor let the circumstance be a motive for hypocrisy. When humility is real, we never leave the state of love, and there is a great sense of belonging, which permits you to do the necessary in every circumstance.

"To be humble is to be loving, to remember our divine origin, and to be faithful to a full life. To be humble is to feel like the stone and the star, the tree and the mountain, the child and the adult . . . and to feel like a child of the Earth and of the Sun, brother of all creation.

"To be humble is always to have a song in your heart, and because of this, what comes out in any situation will unfailingly be tenderness. Ajlla, the Wanderer on the path of the Sun is recognized for the humility that characterizes his actions."

"Chamalú, what happens if I can't be humble every minute?" asked Ajlla.

"You don't need to make an effort to be humble," I told her. "You just need to be well within yourself. If you are, then humility will flow to you spontaneously. Those who are in a prison make their own prison; each one is his own jailer. And with all my heart, I tell you, Ajlla, that the worst thing that can happen to someone is to live in a prison. Find your inner indigenous being; find in yourself that precious condition, your natural condition. Then your body will be filled with eyes, and wherever they look, they will see beauty."

In the last moments, we embraced everything we found: stones, trees, wind, ants, and the invisible elder who accompanied us. Upon leaving, I told her: "Tomorrow at dawn, I will be on the mountain to the south, next to the giant stone. It's important that you come prepared."

"Prepared?" she asked. "Prepared for what, Chamalú?"

"The Wanderer must be prepared for everything, always. Only then does he deserve to live," I said as I left.

The Andean salutation of the Sun is a ceremony of reverence and connection to the light, to Tata Inti, the visible of the invisible God. I worked intensely with it, with the Earth, our mother, and with the guardians of the ancestral tradition. As I finished the ceremony, Ajlla appeared.

"You're just in time," I told her. "Did you salute the guardian stone?"

"Well, I don't think so," she said, blushing.

"Everything is part of you, everything is alive," I continued. "The first intentions and actions upon awakening mark the major tendencies of the day, decide the perspectives, lead to events. While nothing is irreversible, it is difficult to reorient tendencies. It is preferable to pay more attention to the first moments of the day, because with them we print an impression for the rest of the day, until our nightly rest prepares us for the new dawn.

"After asking permission, climb up to the top of the rock. You will find that it is broken in the middle, where it was hit by lightning. This crevice forms a tunnel going down into a cave within. For a long time this was used as a center for ceremony."

"How do you know all this, Chamalú?" asked Ajlla.

"She told me."

"Who?" she asked again.

"Ruba is her name," I said, gesturing toward the huge stone.

"How do rocks speak?"

"Ajlla," I answered while embracing her in a paternal way, "things function differently in each reality. What appears to be false in one reality is true in another. The terms and explanations of one are not valid in another. How do you think our ancestors carried gigantic stones such enormous distances?"

"Can you tell me how it was done?" Ajlla inquired.

"They spoke to them," I responded. "Then the weight was different. Things don't exist only in this reality.

"Climb onto the rock and enter the sacred cave."

Ajlla quickly headed for the rock and tried to climb by one approach after another. Unable to climb it, she returned to my side, saying, "It's impossible to climb, Chamalú. You can tell that there was once a stairway that has been destroyed. It's not possible to climb. Have you been in this cave, Chamalú?"

"No, but I know it."

"I don't understand. If you haven't been there, how can you know it?" asked Ajlla.

"Because Ruba is transparent," I replied.

"Transparent?" she said incredulously, looking at it.

"No, Ajlla, not for these eyes."

"Then for what eyes?"

"You think you can see only with your eyes?" I asked.

"Chamalú," she replied nervously, "every day I understand less."

"You're on the right path," I said, leaving her. "When you get up there, call me."

"But it's impossible to climb."

"Nothing is impossible."

After some time passed, she came to me, sat down, and said, "I can't do it, Chamalú. I tried, and it's impossible."

"Renounce that word that feeds your impotence," I replied. "Did you ask for help from the rock to be able to get to the top?"

"No . . . it didn't occur to me."

"Ajlla," I said slowly. "Reverence and prayer move a lot of energy. You only have to establish a bridge of light between your heart and the center of others; then your request, turned into love, will use the natural laws in a different way. And anyway, you gave up too soon. The Wanderer is the incarnation of the will of stone. He is invincible, immovable, always willing to keep going, advancing in the direction of his fears, feeling at home wherever he is, because he lives in the heart.

"A person without will is like a car without a motor. A stony will is capable of turning every adversity into a sacred challenge, every problem into a teaching, every storm into a stimulus to keep going, being sure that beyond the darkness is once again the light."

"How can I transform myself, Chamalú?"

"The only way to transform yourself is . . . by transforming yourself. Learn everything you are living, without interpreting. To learn from Pachakuty knowledge means unlearning. When you feel that nothing is impossible, when you become what you are doing and focus on the unity of life, you will have begun your new day."

"But living in such a big city as I do, is it possible to do this?" asked Ajlla.

"When you free yourself of inadequate perceptions, you will understand that you are responsible for everything that happens to you.

"The path of the Sun," I continued, "is extensive and varied. To fully live the whole itinerary is the duty of the Wanderer."

"Will we enter the cave?" asked Ajlla.

"You are not yet ready."

"What do I need to do?"

"Stop thinking, Ajlla. You need to stop thinking."

"How can I stop thinking, Chamalú?"

"When you are happy, you think less," I explained. "Also, music and dance open precious spaces of silence."

"Then I need to be dancing or be with music all the time?"

"You've said something very true," I affirmed. "There is music inside all of us. We only have to allow it to flow. Do you think we could live without dancing? Of course not, Ajlla. Dancing is essential. The dance cannot be, should not be, interrupted. Even when we are doing something, the sacred dance must continue. In this way, there is no room for endless thoughts, and so joy will be inevitable."

Later, we shared teachings on the art of walking with reverence and attention. I left her fasting alone, meditating on the teachings of the mountain and of the great rock.

"You will return home when the Sun goes down. When night comes, a star will also be born within you."

Another day had begun. Once more we met in the garden of the same house. Ajlla came each day with a more profound look, a more harmonious expression on her face.

She had come with her hair wet, allowing her almost golden curls to run wild. "Today I asked the water not to be so cold for me, and it heard me. I had the most wonderful time in the shower," Ajlla told me as she arrived.

"How nice to find someone full of joy," I answered her. "When I asked the sacred coca leaves about you last night, they told me that you are a chosen woman, that you had previously shared with us important functions in the conservation of the sacred fire, and for this reason, everything will be easier for you. It is time to go back to your roots. The situation at the moment is urgent, and more Wanderers are needed to fill the path with light."

"Will I really become a Wanderer?" asked Ajlla.

"If you can retain your joy in the worst moments, you are sure to," I answered. "Life is a sacred game, a supreme celebration, a date with plenitude, a wondrous encounter with ecstasy."

"And when things turn out badly?"

"Mistakes are part of learning," I assured her. "What seems bad at the first moment can turn out to be a valuable lesson. However, it is necessary to always be attentive, lucid, and totally present in the moment.

"Being well in the worst moments allows the school of life not to be interrupted. In this context, everything becomes sacred and supreme. These are the moments when we can feel most strongly the reasons why we are on Earth.

"If we are only playing, if it's only a game, Ajlla, then you have the possibility to transform your life into an immensely beautiful sequence and to fly very high, till you reach the heart of the Sun. You have the possibility to enjoy intensely everything that happens. When we enjoy absolutely everything, we learn how to learn and simultaneously how to unlearn. That's when the interior and the exterior become the same, and we can taste the precious unity that is our destiny. Ajlla, we're only playing! Only through playing can you reach the light. Those who refuse to play are condemned to live in darkness. To play is the light; to play is the dawn. To play is to stitch with luminous threads each of the moments that Tata Inti presents.

"I have known many people in the Western world who 'go spiritual' and whose faces are totally serious, but natural spirituality is free—it is a celebration. In our communities, each day is a celebration. How can we not celebrate daily, when life is the best manifestation of Tata Inti? How can we not show our thanks with song and dance, with silence and in joy? How can we not become a gift to others, a daily gift? It is all a game, Ajlla. Tata Inti is playing, and the children of the Sun as well. All awakened beings are playing ceaselessly; those who are sleeping become serious, get complicated, burdened, become resentful, become frustrated, commit suicide. Sometimes they gather among themselves to exchange complaints and dishonest flattery.

"But human beings are simple, in a sense. They never stop being children; therefore, they allow themselves, whether they are executives or laborers, professors or students, young or old, to keep on playing. When something turns out well, when they're successful, upon remembering that it's only a game, they avoid anticosmic vanity. When things turn out badly, they remember that it's only a game, and so joy remains, enthusiasm continues, the uninterrupted inner music feeds the permanent dance.

"Ajlla," I said as I stood up, "we've gotten to the point where more words are meaningless, so the only thing left is to play intensely. Never forget, whatever you're doing, that we're only playing. And all of Pachamama participates in the game."

"I want to learn everything all at once," declared Ajlla when we met at the start of the new day.

"I congratulate your willingness," I said, "but everything must follow a natural process. Awakening is gradual at first, something like the dawn, a tempestuous dawn full of lightning and thunder, with flashes of light, of lucidity, on a curved path along a cliff.

"The Wanderer is being prepared for a long journey, an extensive marathon. We can't sprint as though it was just one hundred meters and we wanted to arrive before others; we can't prepare for only some things. It is necessary to be prepared for everything, to make adversities our preferred teacher. Where would we be without problems?

"Ajlla, you must be prepared for the worst. Only in this way will your preparation be complete; only then will you be clothed in invulnerability and power."

"What would be the worst, Chamalú?" asked Ajlla, obviously interested in the subject.

"The Wanderer is prepared for applause and insults," I went on, "for caresses and for stoning. A Wanderer is one who is not seduced by flattery or by money, one who does not seek gratitude or compensation. He is one who acts in the form of closed circles and who does not beg for sentiments, understanding, or approval. Ajlla, your willingness need not be devoured by rushing. To go beyond this world is a true dawning; you must remember that dawn doesn't happen suddenly, and that the arrival of light is irreversible."

"It's just that sometimes I feel stuck," Ajlla explained. "It seems I stop advancing."

"Have confidence in yourself and in Pachamama and enjoy your transformation," I said slowly. "It is fundamental to watch your growth carefully, without forgetting that we are really growing like trees. At first it is necessary to develop strong and deep roots that will allow us to grow from that inner impulse. It is not possible to increase growth from outside ourselves; it is not possible to force one's individual rhythm. In Pachakuty knowledge, we always work through natural processes."

"This is all very different from common language," said Ajlla. "My friends speak of revolution in a very different manner."

"Most people speak of revolution without ever having the courage to revolutionize their lives, which keep them rotten," I said with emphasis. "Revolution that doesn't begin within, purging the inner pollution, ends up in a cheap facade.

"The only true revolutionary is one who has been transformed. The best way to contribute to the revolution is by transforming decrepit structures. Then, more than revolutionizing society, we drop out of the world even while being in it. In this way, our words become songs, our steps become a dance, and we begin to live consciously and simultaneously in all realities.

"Ajlla," I continued after a pause, "the preparation of a Wanderer is basically the preparation of a festival, a sacred multidimensional celebration that repeats every day. This is the context of all growth. The dawn is inevitable; we just need to be awake and willing. For those who remain asleep, the night continues."

"Only the reverent will reach the top of the mountain," I said, beginning the day's lesson. "Some want to go up with trunks full of fears, others haul their cumbersome pedestals of arrogance and pride. All of this is a blatant act of irreverence. No one who is irreverent can get to Janajpacha.

"When we were given a body to navigate in the *chejpacha*—the cosmic order—and to inhabit Pachamama, we were told that everything is sacred, that love is the only way to relate both within and without. The heart is the only window through which to contemplate life. A star guides our passage when our direction is the Intij Inti.

"When you find yourself in a natural sanctuary, take off your shoes, greet the representatives of the mineral, vegetable, and animal kingdoms, and enter into deep silence. Without looking for it, you will be participating in a multicolored dance where each movement, each color, each happening will be a teaching coming to you in the form of lightning flashes."

"What is sacred?" asked Ajlla. "Where does it end?"

"Everything is sacred; everything is part of the larger temple of the divine," I replied. "When you look from your heart, you see beauty everywhere; the most unusual places can be sources of multidimensional beauty and color and can give wondrous teachings.

"Reverence gives us access to the language of the trees, of the mountains, and of the invisible ones; only the reverent can reach Janajpacha."

"Should we value even the badness in others?" asked Ajlla.

"When someone is mistaken," I replied, "we are in the presence of someone who is more or less asleep and who needs our help. The errors of others are valuable lessons, which show us the path not to follow. No one can hurt you as long as you don't have a habit of being a victim or martyr; nothing can bother you because everyone has the right to clean out his garbage as best as he can. The Wanderer has selective permeability; he's completely vulnerable to the transcendent, to the supreme, yet totally invulnerable to the insignificant or foolish.

"Life is a battlefield. Every day we have an appointment with the supreme, and the way in which we go about it is the great challenge. It's not a question of winning, or of avoiding failure; rather, it is about living fully. The weapons that we use mark the perspective; love and beauty, reverence and humor are the arms of the Wanderer-Warrior. Daily life is the context, all time is in the moment, and the enemy is not without.

"Do you understand?" I continued. "The meaning of this incarnation goes beyond normal labor and convention. It is necessary to expand your limits in order to transcend them; thus we become Wanderers."

"Do the Wanderers have to go live with you in the community?" asked Ajlla.

"Of course not," I said firmly. "The Janajpacha community schools are centers of preparation but not places to stay and live. People from all over converge there; they learn and grow, and then they return to their homes and continue the sacred work. Where we are born is not an accident. There is work to be done in those places and circumstances, and you can leave only after that work has been done."

"How can one be well in places where everything is bad, Chamalú?"

"The Wanderer has to be in all sorts of places, especially the worst. His preparation allows him to remain unshakable in the most adverse circumstances. When it is a question of coherence, the power is inevitable, and it arises irrepressibly.

"Coherence on all levels permits the flowering of that latent inner potential that fills us with power. There we can go through the darkest night, for we are channels of light.

"It's very important to be in the worst places, for the sick who need medication are there. The Wanderer, exercising his coherence, has made a commitment to disinterested service with unconditional love. For this to be possible, it is necessary to be properly fortified, because only then will the frustration not infect our spirit. Ajlla, let reverence be your attitude, and coherence your state of being."

"Chamalú," Ajlla enthusiastically exclaimed, "yesterday I was observing myself when there was a big discussion at home, and I saw that my patience really has grown, that I'm stronger than before and can choose my reactions."

"Did you greet the flowers in the garden as you came in?" I asked indifferently.

"Well, I forgot that," Ajlla answered, confused.

"Did you hear the singing of the birds in the tree in front of the house?" I asked.

"No, Chamalú, I'm sorry."

"Were you grateful, upon awakening, for the new day that was being given to you as a gift? Did you choose not to be grateful, not to hear the bird's song, not to see the flowers?"

Ajlla remained silent with lowered eyes. A slight tremble went through her body.

"The goal of your preparation is to transform you into a Wanderer," I explained. "A Wanderer should never cling to the results of his actions, because they are variable and never depend on only one person.

"I also want you to understand the need for not giving too much importance to the gains obtained, because that path leads to arrogance, which interrupts the gestation period of the Wanderer and causes everything to end in a miscarriage.

"We are very important, but never so much so as to allow arrogance to infect our spirit. Free of that illness, we can embody humility, and this will protect us from the pathological tendency to compare ourselves with others, to feel envy, or to humiliate others.

"The Wanderer proceeds in the most varied and adverse circumstances, always with the same security and humility. He doesn't complicate life. Nothing is complicated when our vision is clear. Make your actions circular, totally circular, without holes where you could lose energy, without gratitude or applause. Ajlla, act in the fullest way possible. Close every circle you open, so that the used energy circulates in it without dispersing. This will increase your power."

Ajlla began to cry, lowering her head even further, hiding her face with her abundant hair.

After a prolonged pause I continued. "Ajlla, you

are still so young! I praise your availability, your willingness, your enthusiasm, your growth. I hope that nothing will detain your growth until your feet become wings and you can transcend the narrow limits of this reality.

"I want to see you prepare for the worst. When you can be well in any circumstance, then the Wanderer will have been born. Remember that to be well implies not renouncing tears, but rather being able to keep in the same little box both your laughter and your tears, your strength and your tenderness."

"Was I wrong in telling you what I did?" she asked as she dried her cheeks.

"You were wrong in forgetting what you forgot. You were wrong to arrive here living what had already happened, because in that way you betrayed the present.

"Ajlla, the Wanderer is true to the moment, living it intensely, because he knows that it is his school, his passport to eternity."

"And it wasn't good the way I behaved," insisted Ajlla.

"Your attitude is wonderful, but what isn't right is the importance you give to what you did," I explained. "When we value the results of our actions too much, we become dependent on them, and this subordination keeps us from enjoying what we are doing, because we will be too preoccupied with the results. Understand? Basically, I'm speaking about the preservation of your freedom. You can't change it for a handful of praise, because praise is addictive, and you'll end up doing things to please others."

"How can I be free, Chamalú?"

"Freedom is the most beautiful gift we have been given," I answered. "In times like these, to be free means to have fewer and fewer needs; then you will be less obliged to sell your life for a little money. To be free means to live free of fear, which in truth is not necessary. To be free implies renouncing self-deception, fanaticism, and intolerance. Ajlla, there is no noise of chains near a Wanderer. No prison, no matter how comfortable it may seem, is visited by him.

"When one still lacks knowledge, one tends to buy lots of things, to consume a lot, to run a lot. When the Sacred Wisdom is incorporated into our lives, however, sobriety, austerity, and frugality spontaneously become part of our lives, freeing us from many camouflaged chains. Then a silent voice will teach us that it is not necessary to be attached to anything, that all dependence is a prison, that it is not possible to fly from a cage.

"Ajlla, preserve the jewel of freedom no matter what the cost. Become an untamable warrior when they try to encroach upon your freedom. Become permeable to the transcendent and invulnerable to foolishness, to flattery and applause, to insults and aggressions. You were born free, and you have the duty to leave this world *free!*"

16

At the beginning of the day's lesson, I said, "We are basically energy beings. We need energy in order to function, and we receive it from the Earth when we walk, from the air when we breathe, from the foods we eat, from Tata Inti when we meditate, from the trees when we embrace them, and from the fire when we dance."

"There are that many ways of nourishing ourselves?" asked Ajlla. "I thought it was only through eating and breathing."

"We don't live only from oxygen and food," I explained. "We also need other invisible sources of nourishment, which we receive upon entering in contact with different elements. For city dwellers, it's highly important to go to the country as often as possible, to allow Tata Inti, after dawn or before setting, to caress our skin. Noon is the best moment to connect with the Earth and the stones, either directly or through thin clothing of natural fibers. In this way, our appetite for energy is satiated. Music, silence, rain, and starlight all form part of the varied menu for energy.

"At one time," I continued, "during the invasions of our people, an elder native was captured and left for days tied to a tree, in the courtyard of the military barracks. His oppressors purposely forgot to provide him with food, because they wanted to see him suffer and die of hunger, begging for food. But that's not what happened. Days and weeks went by as the old man remained unchanged, his appearance increasing in health and radiance. He lacked digestive foods, but he was fed from abundant sources. Do you understand? He was nourished constantly, although his captors were not aware of it.

"Referring to digestive foods, I would say that a fruit or a cereal provides us not so much with what the biochemistry registers as with invisible proteins, vitamins of light, which are plentiful in foods cultivated not with chemical products but with reverence and love. In the same way, medicinal plants help more on a subtle level than through elements discovered in laboratories. A true healer sees the light in plants and connects with the vibration of each one. In this way, he or she establishes an energetic bridge with the vegetable kingdom."

"So eating is a lot more important than we imagine," affirmed Ajlla.

"It is wonderful to see those who eat with gratitude

and respect. Each piece of fruit is the result of a multidimensional community labor, to which is added the labor of humans. For a Wanderer, to eat is a meditation. During meals he establishes a bridge of light with the vegetable kingdom; then, if the context is adequate, magic flows, and on the subtle level he is nourished in all his bodies.

"It is important to prepare foods with love, to treat them with respect and gratitude, to energize them before eating. Conscious nutrition is important—to be attentive, as though you were speaking to the spirit of each item. It is fundamentally important to cultivate foods with tenderness, relating to the Earth from levels of reciprocity and love. There are indigenous farmers who, while planting, don't allow anyone who is angry or sad to walk upon that land; they say that such a presence would 'ruin the soil.' By contrast, these farmers like to take children to play on the land before cultivating it, because innocence is a powerful energy, purity a valuable fertilizer—for the Earth, as well as for plants and humans."

"Chamalú, what foods do I need, and what should I avoid?"

"Meditate in order to hear your own body," I answered. "Speak to each part constantly, and then you will feel what is needed without fear of making mistakes. It is important in times of world famine to opt for a diet that permits others to eat daily—that is to say, to eat a frugal vegetarian meal.

"Our nourishment also needs to be at the same level of evolution as ourselves, becoming more subtle as we do. All growth refers to the total person. That's why it is important to speak to our bodies in a context of respect and gratitude. As for the rest, the future days will teach us in time.

"Each food is a celebration, a dance of tastes and enthusiasm. The Wanderer intensely enjoys everything he eats because he knows that it is part of the sacred ceremony that provides us with the combustion necessary to go on.

"Ajlla, each meal is a date with Pachamama."

17

"There is something I've wanted to ask you for days but have not dared," Ajlla said after the usual morning greeting. "I don't know how to say it, as it refers more or less to the theme of couples. I've never been with a boy, although I've had plenty of opportunities . . . maybe because of the influence of my parents, I don't know. What I want to know is if, with the training I'm receiving now, I'm obliged to remain alone, or . . . I don't know. Do you understand?"

"The formation of the Wanderer-Warrior is the development and birth of an authentic human being, fulfilled and clothed in light. A Wanderer can be a monk, an *amauta* (a wise one), a healer, a teacher; in each phase you can find various formulas, but the essence is the same.

"Ajlla, it's worthwhile to be alone without feeling

lonely when the company is not adequate or when the person at your side is a hindrance. It's only worthwhile to enjoy a partner when it's possible to grow together and in freedom."

"I don't want anything to interfere with my growth, Chamalú," Ajlla answered firmly. "I've had some brief friendships, but they were so superficial that sometimes I felt bad not to be alone."

"A Wanderer decides each of his actions," I went on. "Always act from your heart, and then it won't be based on what others will say. Your purity guarantees your actions. When you say yes, it will be because your whole body is filled with that affirmation. When you refuse, it will be conclusive and loving—never a victim, never a tyrant.

"Our ancestors, the Incas, used the *tantanacuy* (premarital practice), so that all couples could know each other before making a decision. And the only way to know each other is to share adversities. Bad times are a good school; the rest is often a lie."

"Is it better to grow alone or with a partner?"

"Growth is always personal," I replied. "With a good partner, however, you can do very interesting work. What is totally absurd is to try to climb the mountain carrying a coffin. To choose well is essential; otherwise, solitude is preferable from any point of view.

"One way to recognize your potential partner is to see if you preserve your liberty in all ways. Any attempt to compromise your freedom is a bad sign, which will indicate that the person is inadequate company. Of course, one should first speak about all this, establishing a clear and flexible agreement, setting limits that both consider necessary, and then moving within that open space, with love and total freedom. Then growth will be assured, trust will be real, and the differences will enrich the union. Compassion, tolerance, respect are flowers cultivated in the garden of tenderness. Freedom becomes an impressive tree, in whose branches the birds will sing their loveliest songs.

"Ajlla, each situation comes at its own time and circumstance. It is not good to force processes or to look for them. The Wanderer doesn't seek anything, acting with disinterest and attention. He is an explorer of himself and his surroundings. His intuition becomes like a sense of smell. He senses at every moment what is necessary."

"What do I need right now?"

"You need to learn to walk, Ajlla," I answered, "and when your feet become wings, you can fly high. Then your vision will have increased, and you will see deeply; choose adequately and keep flying. What you need at this time, Ajlla," I went on, "is to enjoy intensely this precious age you have, increase your resources, fill your days with love until you are clothed in light. Then darkness will dissolve in your presence, and you will be a gift to others.

"Ajlla, life is too beautiful to lose it because of faulty

decisions. Without freedom we become prisoners. What good is it if they fill the prison with comforts and gifts, if the door is closed? What good is love that chains or stifles you? Tata Inti wants to see all his children free, flying toward the light.

18

"Ajlla, tonight you are going to die." I surprised her with this announcement as she arrived. Shocked and confused, she looked at me, then lowered her eyes as they filled with tears, for she surely hadn't expected this.

There was a long silence before I continued.

"The Wanderer must be prepared for anything, especially so death does not find him in a place of mistaken attitude.

"Ajlla, death always walks at our side wherever we go. It is our permanent companion, but it need not worry us or cause fear. Death walks at our side to remind us that we must live."

"Is it possible to avoid the fear of death?"

"The fear of death is justified only for those who are

not in their place. For one who is living fully and from the heart, death is truly a gift, the dawning of a new day, the birth to a new life."

"What about the suffering when you die, Chamalú?" asked Ajlla. "Dying is very painful."

"It is possible that in many cases it is painful for the body, but for the spirit it is a liberation. Truly, there is nothing to fear. Have you forgotten that we are eternal?"

"Chamalú, what happens after death?"

"What is important to know," I replied, "is what happens before dying. Where do your steps take you each day? How do you fill the hours? You must appropriately experience the itinerary that continues until your death. All I can say for now is that the process is wonderful and there is nothing to fear, although it is fundamental to be prepared."

"What does it mean to be prepared, Chamalú?"

"The best preparation is a full life," I affirmed. "The Wanderer works in circles, never leaving a circle open. By closing everything you open, nothing is left pending, so it's the same to die today, tomorrow, or in a year.

"To close the circle means to act fully. If you make a mistake, admit it and overcome it. If the error is someone else's, understand him and forgive him. There are no holes, no wounds, no room for resentment or anger. The circle is closed; the confluence of the action and the intention preserve the energy. Everything circles in ascendant spirals—that is the movement of life."

"How can we avoid the fear of death?"

"You have only to be in your proper place, enjoying each instant, tasting each moment, learning from every situation. Ajlla, we die every night, we resurrect every morning.

"When you awaken, you should say, 'I'm alive again!' When you go to bed, you should leave everything clearly and harmoniously concluded, so if you do not wake up in the morning, nothing will be pending.

"Ajlla, never go to sleep without having forgiven and forgotten, without having freed yourself of negative thoughts or feelings, without being grateful for the day you were given. When you wake up, decide to be happy just for today because only today is real, only today are you alive, only today can you love and enjoy. We only have one day, each day."

"Should I remember that death is always at my side?"

"Only when it is necessary," I replied, "and to give strength to the intensity of your life, of your hours, so that not a minute goes by in vain, so that you are fully alive throughout the day, and so that when death finds you, it does not find you already dead.

"Live fully, for life is the best idea God ever had, and it should be celebrated."

19

When Ajlla arrived, we went out to the courtyard and greeted the tree and then the flowers. We went back to the tree, a huge willow, and taking a branch in each hand, I said to Ajlla, "Let us dance with the Wasimasillay. He is a brother—he has always been here, and let us celebrate that."

And a song in an indigenous language gradually filled the space and our bodies, allowing, in the midst of the dance, access to other realities: light, intense colors, the absence of separation between all and everything, irrepressible joy.

How long did we remain like this? Who is the tree, on the deepest levels? Finally, at the end, Ajlla shared her moving experience.

"It's incredible, Chamalú. What I experienced is so incredible that words seem incapable of describing it.

"When you began to sing," she continued, "I felt as though the Earth opened and received me. I saw that its interior isn't dark but full of light. I came back from within the Earth and saw myself dancing with the tree, except that the tree had a face. There was so much light, so much color. I looked toward where you were, but in place of you I saw an old man. In another moment, for an instant, I saw a circle of ancient ones surrounding us, men and women, dancing and singing. But when I looked again, almost in fear, they disappeared. I don't know, but I thought the tree was a person; it seemed to watch me continuously. Chamalú! Is it real, what I saw?"

"Ajlla, I told you once, there are things that aren't true in this reality but are totally real in the other reality—which is just as real as this one, except that your normal senses don't have the capacity to include them."

We went back to our usual place, after taking leave of the tree. There I continued. "I wanted you to know the force and the beauty of Andean music and dance. They serve as passports to other realities, as activators to inner processes, as resounding hallucinogens, immensely pleasurable. They feed processes in a totally natural way.

"Song, music, and dance," I continued, "are powerful ways of meditation and harmonization; typical working tools for the Wanderer. They are doors to other realities that are also here. Our ancestors united them with the fire, with the sacred bonfire. In a context of total reverence the Universe was recreated, and Pachamama danced in multidimensional faces.

"It is in circumstances like these that we completely stop normal mental sequences, allowing access to a common language spoken by all beings.

"Ajlla, work deeply with music, song, and dance, every minute, everywhere, and your levels of intuition will heighten. When intuition is freed, we discover that we are not alone, that we don't need to think or calculate too much, that a deeper vision flows within us, that we can feel what we must do in any circumstance. The Wanderer, by purifying his body and opening his heart, by being loving, reverent, and whole, will know from his increased intuition where he belongs, will recognize his path, and will proceed without hesitation. Little by little his actions, no matter how small, become true works of art, luminous complete circles; the sacred mantel of life becomes woven with the vocation of a multidimensional artist. Life itself becomes a sacred work of art. Ajlla, only sensitive artists, who make their lives a precious work of art, will discover the Janajpacha. The Wanderer is a supreme artist. He knows that he is at every moment performing the sacred labor of building and polishing himself."

"Can we all become artists of the sacred?" Ajlla asked.

"The construction of our supreme work of art," I

assured her, "is an evolutionary growth process, which indicates the transcendental meaning of our passage on the Earth in this body. Tata Inti is an artist, and the spiritual guides are artisans of the invisible. The making of our lives into a sacred work of art is the path of returning to the source, hand in hand with beauty."

20

"Is money evil?" Ajlla opened the day's meeting with this question.

"Nothing is good or evil in itself; everything is an opportunity," I answered. "Money is evil when it becomes your fundamental objective, your priority, when you stop living fully in order to obtain it, when you confuse it with happiness. However, when money is a working tool that you manage with disinterest and intelligence, without dependence or obsession, but in the service of your evolution, then there is no reason for it to be bad.

"The problem resides not in having or not having money, but in lacking knowledge and wisdom, because then misuse is guaranteed. A good example of this is the world and its injustices. Those who don't share go against their own evolution. Spirituality is synonymous not with poverty but with coherence and love, and these can be found in the most diverse circumstances."

"And those who work only for money, aren't they headed toward evil?"

"When money is our only objective, then no matter what we do, we're out of the sacred path. But it's also necessary to be in all places. What's important is authenticity, purity, elevated goals, understanding.

"The Wanderer isn't a refugee, someone who evades society. That's why he can be found in all places, in the most diverse occupations; his invincibility is the guarantee. His presence counters low tendencies and opens spaces of light, even without saying anything. His fulfilled presence is a valuable point of reference.

"Ajlla," I went on, "the Wanderer needs to know how to live in all realities, with the same fullness, coherence and love. Then waves of peace and oceans of harmony will flow from within him. The look in his eyes will be peaceful and serene in any circumstance; all his actions will be inspired by tenderness."

"Is that what happiness is?" asked Ajlla.

"Happiness is our natural state," I answered. "That is to say, unhappiness is an affront to the Universe, an act of irreverence to Tata Inti, a grotesque pollution of the atmosphere. We have no right to be unhappy. It is an infraction."

"Chamalú, is it possible always to be happy?"

"As it is our natural state of being, happiness flows

spontaneously when we stop complicating things, when we see everything as a challenge, as a teaching, as an opportunity to keep growing. How can one be unhappy in the midst of so much beauty? Look at any starlit night, contemplate the sunrise.

"If we observe so many people who are unhappy, we have all the more reason to be happy, because the only thing we can do for them is to be well."

"Even when things are going badly?" asked Ajlla.

"Especially when things go badly," I answered. "When everything is going well, there is no merit in being well—any idiot can manage that. It is a question of being at peace during the storms, the adversities, in the worst circumstances.

"Ajlla, we are condemned to be happy."

"Ajlla"—I took her hands in mine when she arrived for the day's encounter—"I'm leaving in two days. You no longer need me. After tomorrow, you will have to continue on your path alone."

"I'll miss you very much, Chamalú," she said with a sadness she could not hide. "Can't I go with you?"

"The Wanderer does only what is absolutely necessary," I answered her. "You won't be alone. Even though your physical eyes see nothing, you will be accompanied. Ajlla, we miss only that which, even if physically with us, is not present. My presence will stay with you, because I am not outside of you. How can you miss me? First, you would have to 'tear me out' of yourself, don't you think?

"We'll see each other again in the future, in full flight. When I met you, you were a little worm crawling on the ground with difficulty. Your opportunity

92

came in the form of a problem. Where would you be without your problems? Now your wings are growing; your flight awaits you."

"Will I be able to do it alone, Chamalú?"

"I promise you that your wings are sufficient for you," I reassured her. "The Wanderer is powerful when his habitual state of mind is understanding. Remember that therein comes the power that will clothe you in light.

"Ajlla, silence is the language of the Wanderer. Each time you enter total silence, you have access to the language of all beings. Then you will be able to communicate with the trees and the rocks, with the moon and the mountains, with the animals and the flowers, with the guardians of the Earth and Tata Inti.

"Speak with everything, for everything has life; find in everything an older or younger brother. Everything is one, everything is alive."

I invited her to lie down with her head to the east, following the sacred sound of the *zampoña* and the *zanca* (large panpipes). I led her to a level of deep rest. From there we took a journey, first connecting with our power animal. We traveled to the rhythmic, monotonous sound of first a maraca, then a drum. We were transformed into birds, flew over the present, and visited the past, traveling along the path of time.

The sensations became reality. Ajlla had been here before. How many of those who are spontaneously attracted to the indigenous have been our ancestors?

The voyage was wondrously beautiful. When we returned, Ajlla started to cry uncontrollably. From then on, no words were necessary. Just tears, which made her expression more lovely, as well as caresses and a profound silence coming from a transparent peace, which became a crystalline drop, a sacred lake, an ocean of multidimensional unity. I asked her to come early the next day. We would go to the nearby mountain, where we would meet for the last time.

22

We met ascending the mountain, under the departing stars.

"We must always remain in the sacred circle." With these words, I began the day's lesson without interrupting our ascent. "The air one breathes in the circle is love; there we are protected and accompanied. But when we leave the circle, the protection leaves us, and we become vulnerable. Outside the circle, any thought or decision that does not correspond with our essence is better avoided.

"Our personal rainbow fills only our circle; outside it, direct communication with Tata Inti is interrupted. When you discover that you are outside the circle, avoid justifications and self-delusion. What is needed is to forgive yourself and forgive others and be willing to return to the circle. Outside it, nothing has meaning.

Outside your sacred circle are darkness and confusion. When you find yourself there, return with humility, learning from the circumstances."

"Will you teach me a ritual, Chamalú?"

"Life itself is a sacred ritual, a supreme ceremony," I answered. "In it everything is important, because it moves not only in this reality. In the second part of your formation, you will enter into the world of magic in a very deep way. First, it is important for you to digest everything we have been working on together, integrating it into your own daily routine, moving through the world without being part of it. For the Wanderer, everything is a temple; every act is sacred. That's why being whole is the only way to be in this life."

We arrived at the entrance of a lovely cave and asked permission to enter. Once authorized, we went inside the cave and began preparing Ajlla for her first initiation.

Time became circular. The sacred fire presented itself in all its strength, the heartbeat of the Earth fused with the sound of the ceremonial drum, and the purified water, prepared with white petals that had previously been blessed, ran over her body, restoring its purity, empowering her innocence, increasing her transparency. There was a profound silence, a luminosity that did not come from the dawning day. Tata Inti arrived to join in the sacred act. The silence was decorated with song; the incense, the *koa* (a sacred plant), and the offering of coca leaves symbolized the sacred reciprocity.

The hours passed in circular fashion. There was such a concentration of energy that each step, each moment, each gesture left a shower of light. Each word left a prolonged reverberation. Time had stopped. The gift of a spherical quartz crystal closed the ceremony. We took leave of the ancestors who had accompanied us, and we gave thanks to the mountain that had received us in her breast. Slowly, we returned outside. Ajlla continued to chant her song as tears of emotion wet her cheeks. When we finally left, it was close to noon. We started down the mountain . . . my last words were left to hear.

"Ajlla, as of today, the name you received will vibrate in your frequency. *Ajlla* means 'chosen.' You have been chosen to fulfill a job of great importance in the world; your preparation must intensify. Remember the importance of beginning the day with gratitude. When you wake up, salute the day with a smile and be willing to delight in this new gift with totality. As you get out of bed and take your first steps, remember that you are an unstoppable Wanderer.

"Observe how each day has its own dawning. Rise with the day; begin it renewed, reborn. Be reborn each day, renewed to displace the darkness and fill it with light. When you are outside with Tata Inti, spark your inner light. As you wash daily, remember the fluidity of water. As you wash your body, purify yourself within. Before dressing, caress your body; speak to it! When you dress, remember the importance of beauty, enjoy decorating your body, rather than dressing as a way to hide the shame it produces in you. In each act, in each thought, remain in the circle of love, where a powerful, concentrated energy builds an invisible wall of protection.

"Always be grateful. Embody tenderness at the worst times. Your battlefield is where you find yourself. Your school is life. Your instructors are the problems that arise. Everything is an opportunity to keep growing. Fortify your body. Train yourself to feel comfortable in the most diverse circumstances. Find refuge periodically in the Earth, or in the forests. When energizing yourself, do not be demanding; share through your presence, sing often, dance everywhere. If others think you are crazy, confirm their suspicions; that way they will leave you alone once and for all. Forgive freely. Share. Happiness multiplies when you share. Love everything you do, enjoy life continuously, take intense pleasure in living. Wanderers are in love with a fulfilled life, and they are faithful to it."

After descending the mountain, we said good-bye warmly. Ajlla had a transparent look in her eyes; she looked fulfilled. She tried to say something more, but no words passed her lips. As so many times in the past, she hid her face in her abundant, sun-colored hair. My last words signaled our taking leave of one another.

"This is a beginning more than an ending. Ajlla, the festival of your life has just begun. There will be other steps, other initiations, profound experiences, pathways closer to the Sun. Will you be ready for these new challenges that will expand your growth? If you are, then our guides will stay at your side, dressed in transparency.

"May the immense strength of Pachamama protect you and the purifying light of Tata Inti enlighten your way. *Munakuyki*—I love you."

Epilogue

Half a millennium has passed since the destruction of the Inca Temples of the Sun. Through the hands of the indigenous spiritual guide Chamalú, the first modern *intiwasi*, or Temple of the Sun, was built and opened to the world. It is destined to contribute to multiracial and spiritual sharing. These are times for unity in diversity. Intentions and words are no longer sufficient.

Soon, other *intiwasis* will be created in the jungle and in the Andes of Bolivia, within spiritual initiatory communities. These will open to the entire world access to the sacred knowledge of the Andes and the mystical teachings of the jungle. They also will allow for the living experience of this surprisingly magical natural spirituality, free of dogma, sectarianism, or complications.

In the communities, people will work with the sacred fire, shamanic voyages, ecstatic dances, ceremonial music, and initiatory tales. There will also be profound cures, purifying experiences, meditations in places of power, indigenous teachings, and ancestral architecture. They are open to all who seek the sacred.

Travel to Bolivia

Janajpacha, a spiritual community and school, was inaugurated on June 21, 1993. It is situated in the valley of Cochabamba, in central Bolivia.

The majestic *intiwasi*, a new Temple of the Sun, is situated in this community. It is the first to be opened in the West in this new Pachacuti.

In the community, as though sprouted from the Earth, are various circular dwellings built in an indigenous style, combining mud, stone, bamboo, and Andean grasses. They create an agreeable setting for rest and the renewal of energy.

This shamanic community is a few kilometers from the guardian mountain, close to ancient thermal waters, and halfway between the Andes and the jungle. It is an authentic natural sanctuary, where inner growth is stimulated and other realities are presented with undeniable intensity.

It has been designed to receive temporarily all seekers of light and to offer continuous encounters, seminars and courses, festivals and ceremonies, and dances and pilgrimages.

Those interested should write to

> Chamalú
> Casilla 318 Correo Central
> Cochabamba
> Bolivia

Glossary

Amauta   Andean shaman; guide; guardian of the Sacred Wisdom.

Intij Inti   Supreme cosmic energy, God.

Janajpacha   Heaven, superior reality. Also the name of the Andean initiatory communities in the jungles and mountains of Bolivia.

Kaypacha   Present reality.

Pachacuti   Era or cycle; cyclic period of time of variable duration; time with its own specific characteristics.

Pachakuty   The teachings that Chamalú shares with the West, as well as the communities known by the name of Pachakuty knowledge.

Pachamama   Mother Earth; also, the universe.

Tata Inti   Father Sun; visible representation of the Invisible God.